LYNNE PICKERING

ART

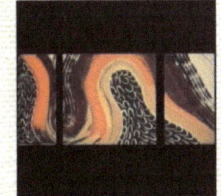

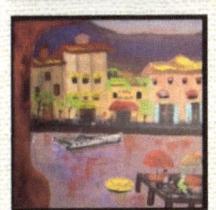

& INTERIORS

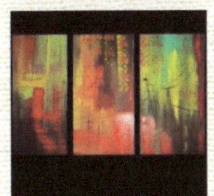

Lynne Pickering   Copyright

ISBN NUMBER 13: 9781503183117

ISBN 10 :1503183114

CREATE SPACE

ART by Lynne Pickering

BOOK DESIGN LYNNE PICKERING

TABLE OF CONTENTS

CHAPTER 1   BEACH THEMES   PAGE 4-20

CHAPTER 2   FLOWERS   PAGE 21- 24

CHAPTER 3   AUSTRALIAN   PAGE 25-31

CHAPTER 4   QUIRKY   PAGE 32-35   GROUP PICTURES

CHAPTER 5   ABSTRACT   PAGE 36-37

CHAPTER 5   LANDSCAPE   PAGE 36-40

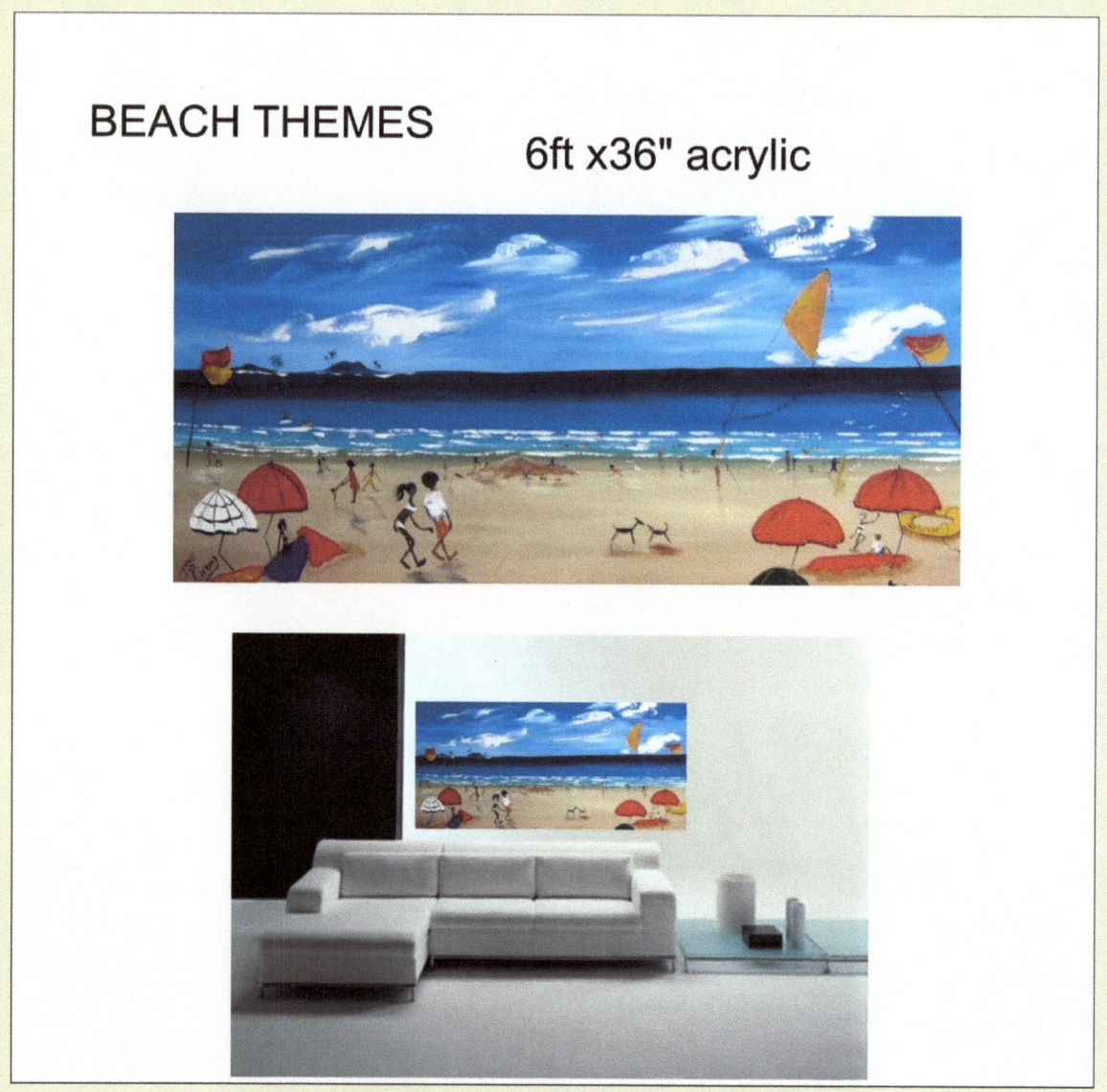

BEACH THEMES

6ft x36" acrylic

BEACH THEMES

4 PANELS   80CMX40CM = 1.6 MTRS WIDE

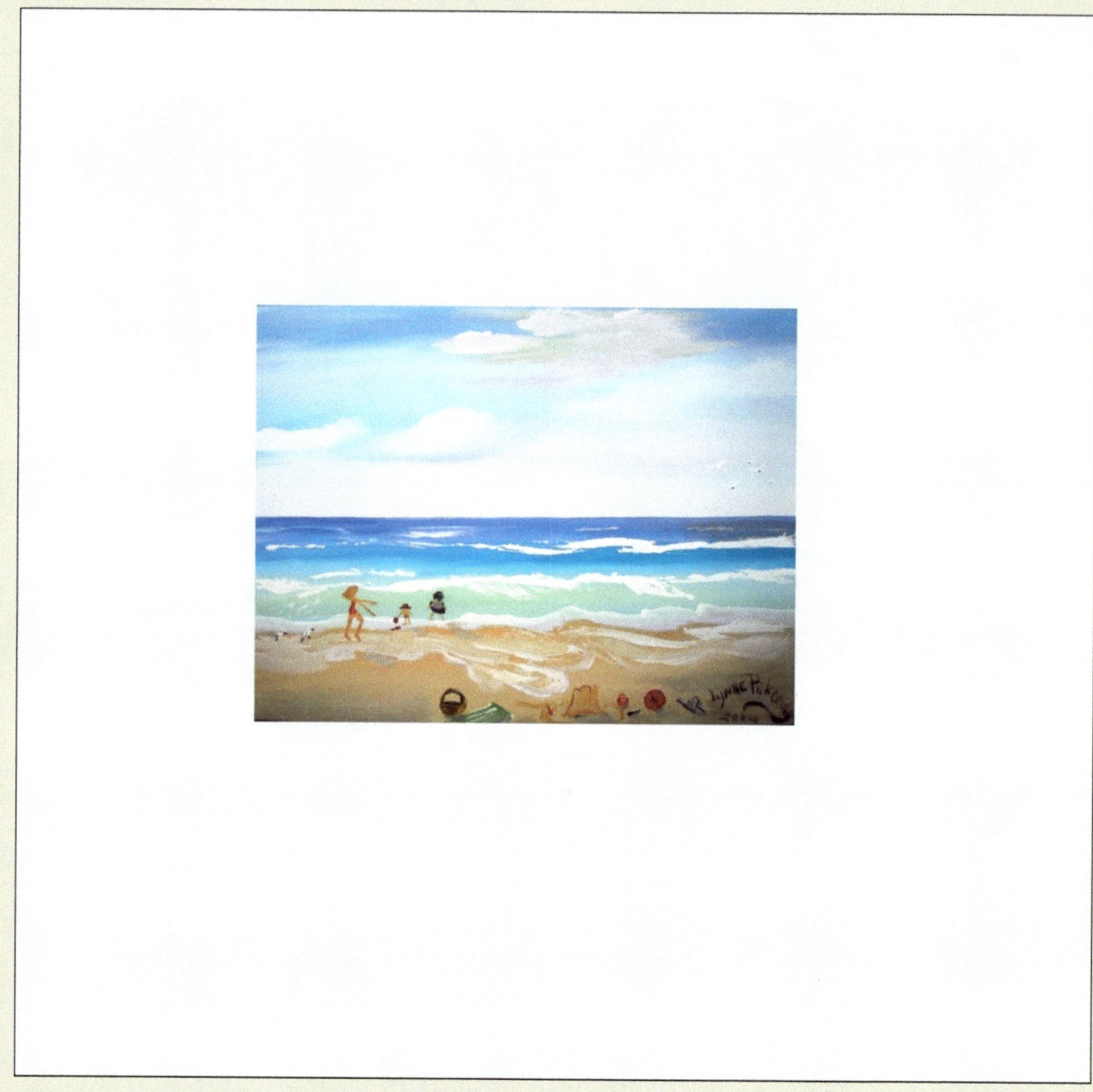

BEACH THEMES   48"X24"

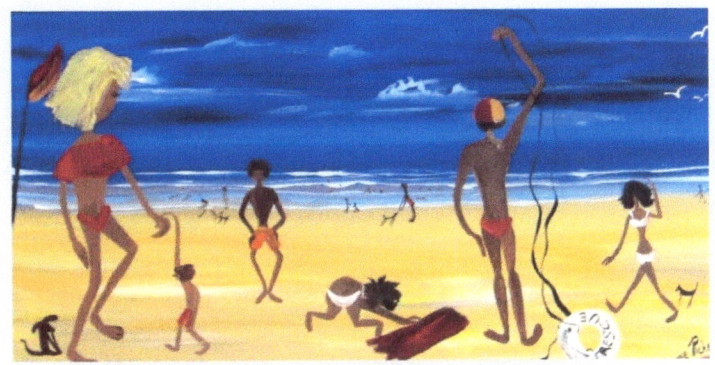

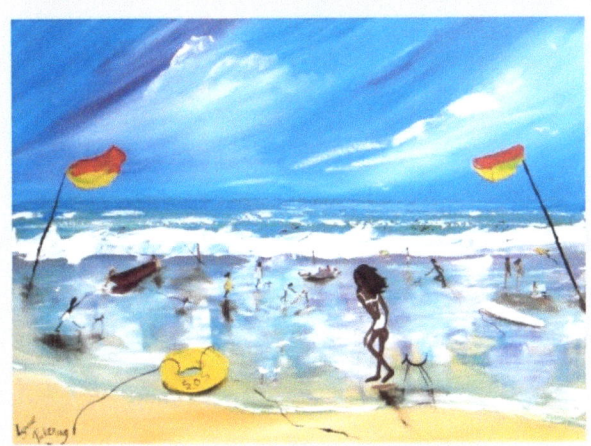

48x36" acrylic

BEACH THEMES 48"X24" acrylic

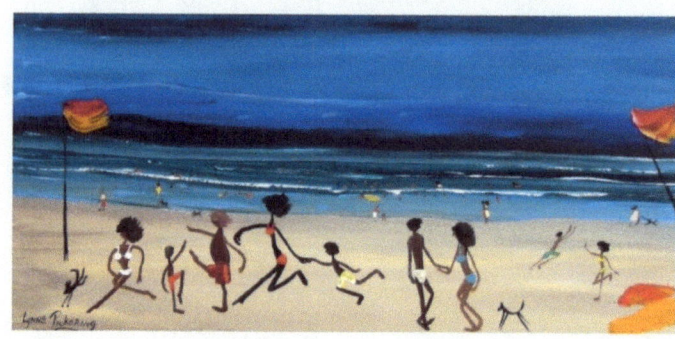

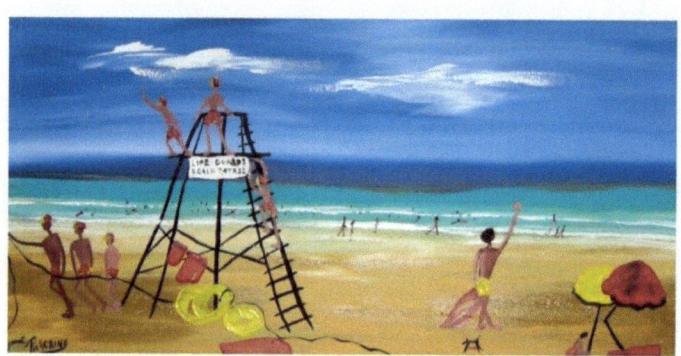

BEACH THEMES

48"X48" acrylic
Abstract Saturday Beach

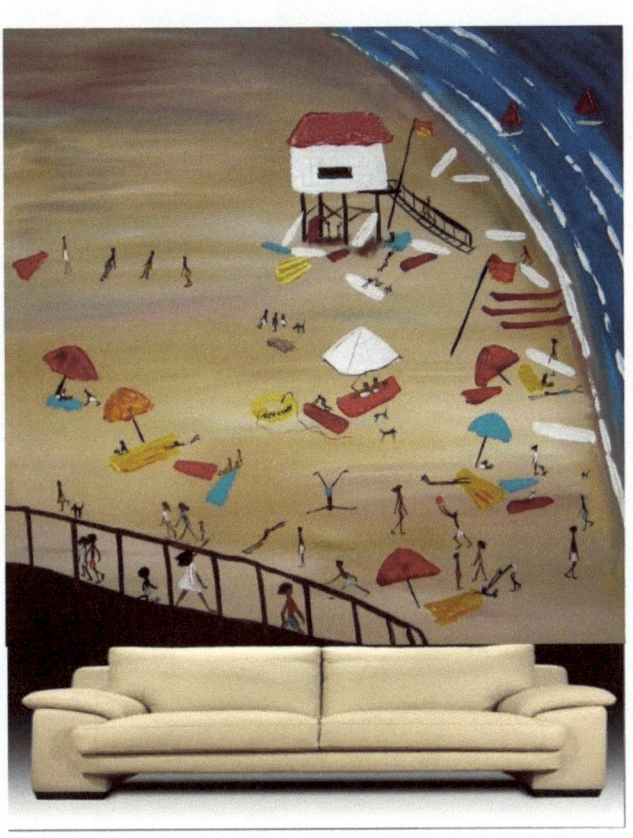

BEACH THEMES

5ft x40" acrylic beach
stormy sky

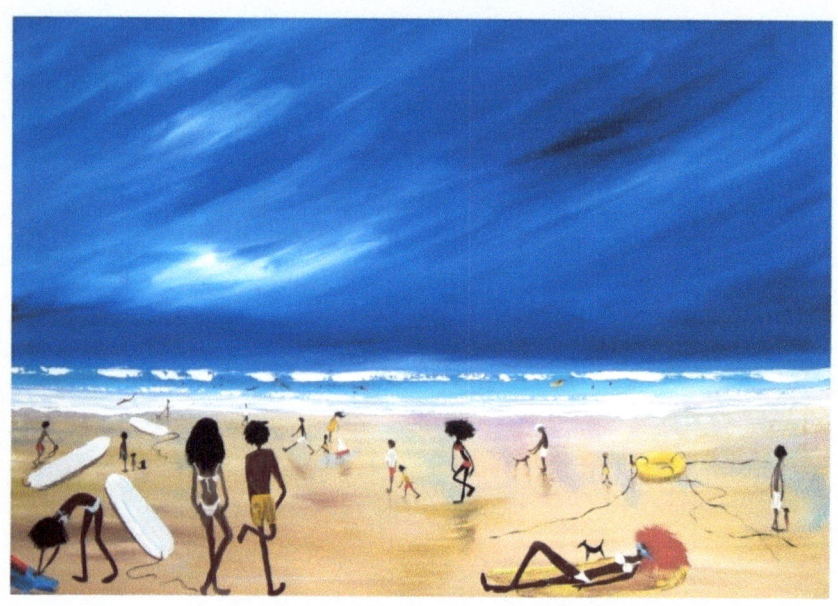

BEACH THEMES   48"X48" acrylic
Abstract Beach

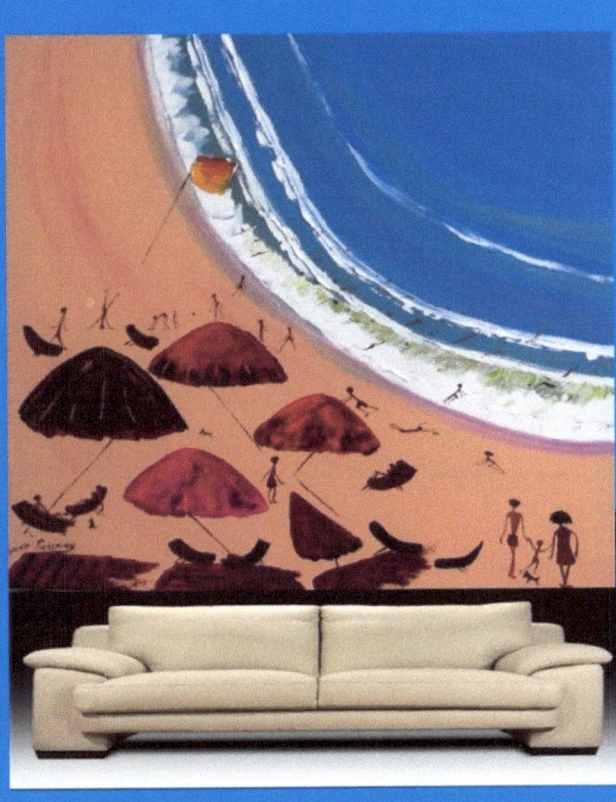

BEACH THEMES   48X48" ACRYLIC

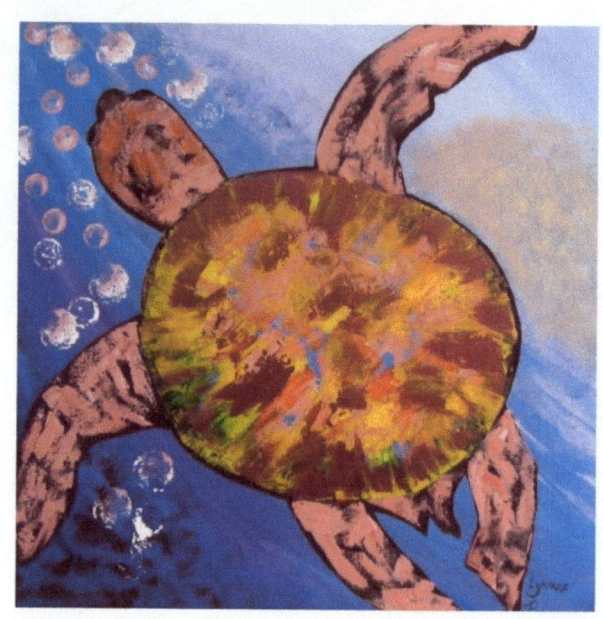

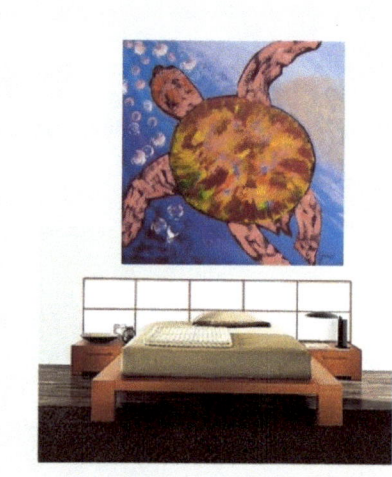

BEACH THEMES   54"X40" acrylic
Abstract KITE Beach

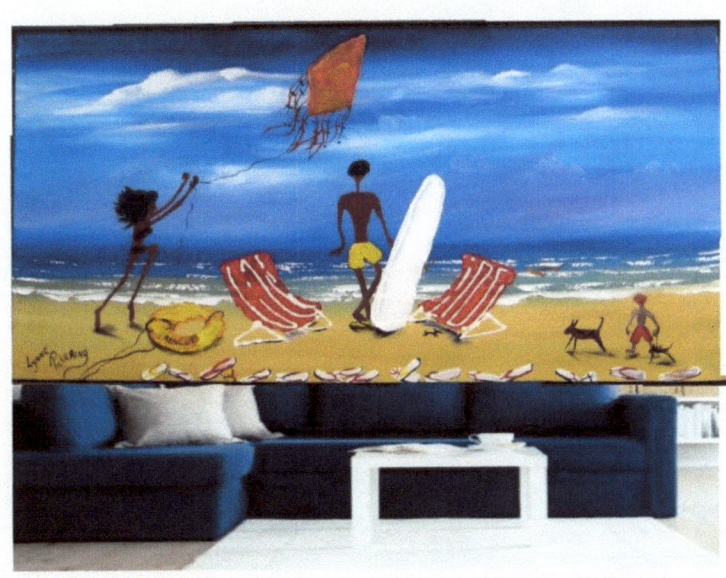

BEACH THEMES   36"X36" acrylic

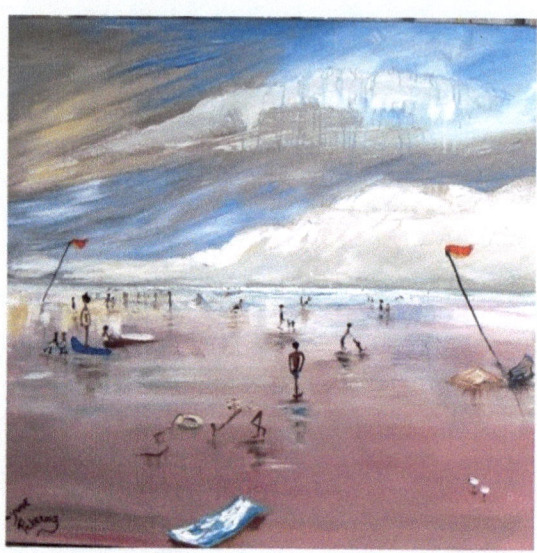

UNDERWATER JELLYFISH 36"x36"

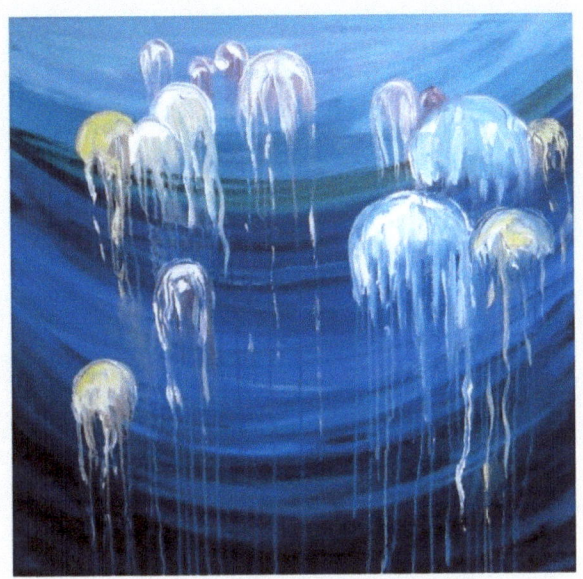

BEACH GIRLS 48"X24"

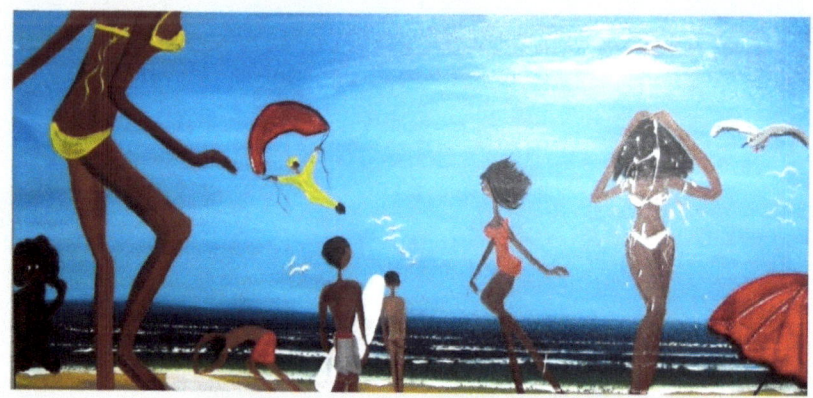

BEACH THEMES 48"X36"

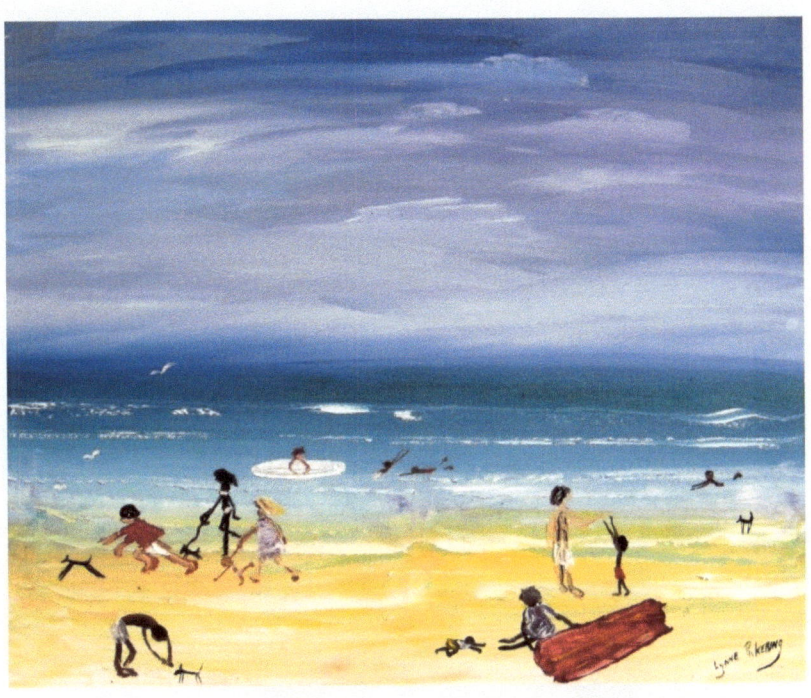

PARTY GIRLS 36" X24" ACRYLIC

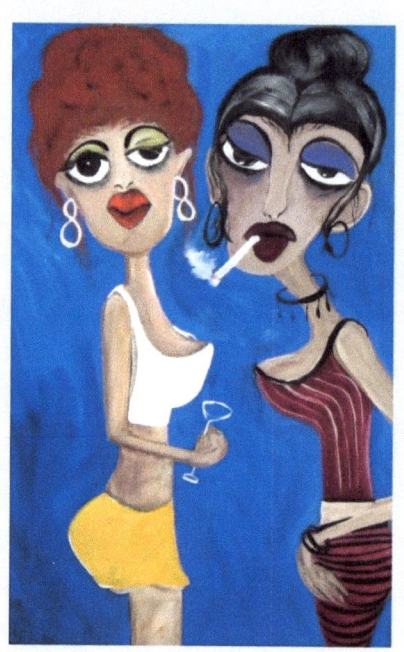

BEACH PARTY   36"X24" ACRYLIC

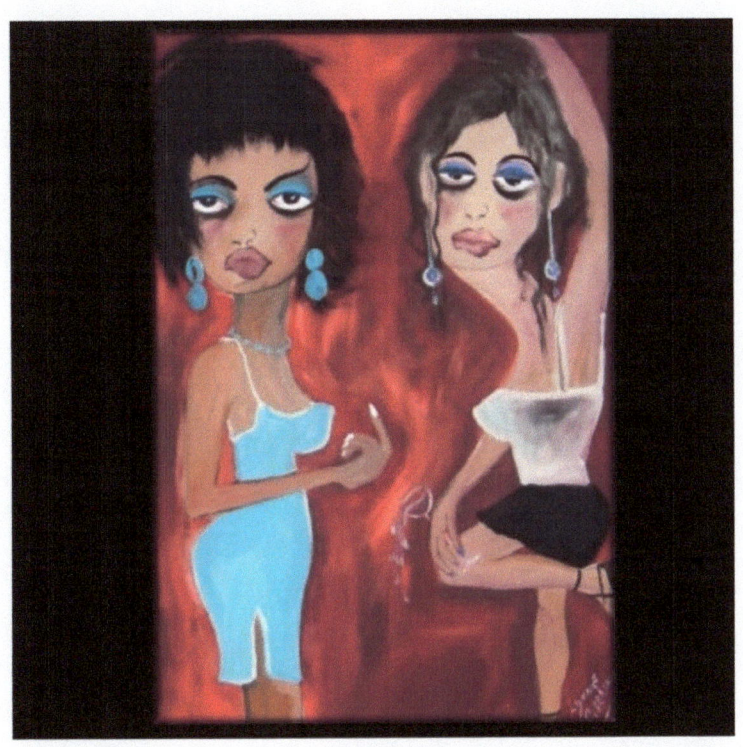

PARTY GIRLS 36"X24"

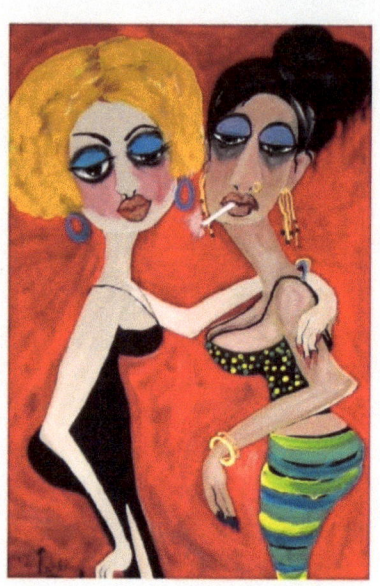

Floral art   red poppies 36 "x36"

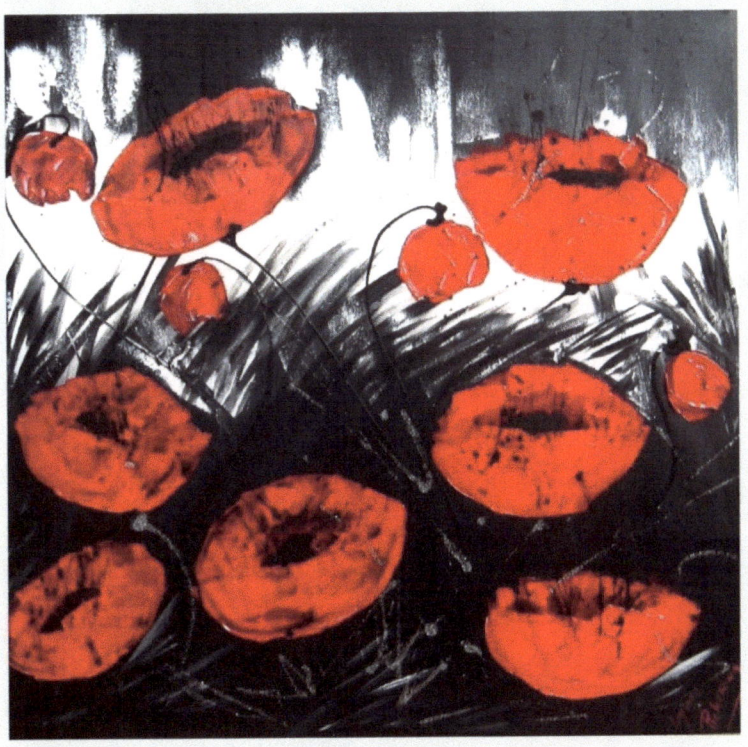

Massive Frangipani 1.8 mtrs x45cm

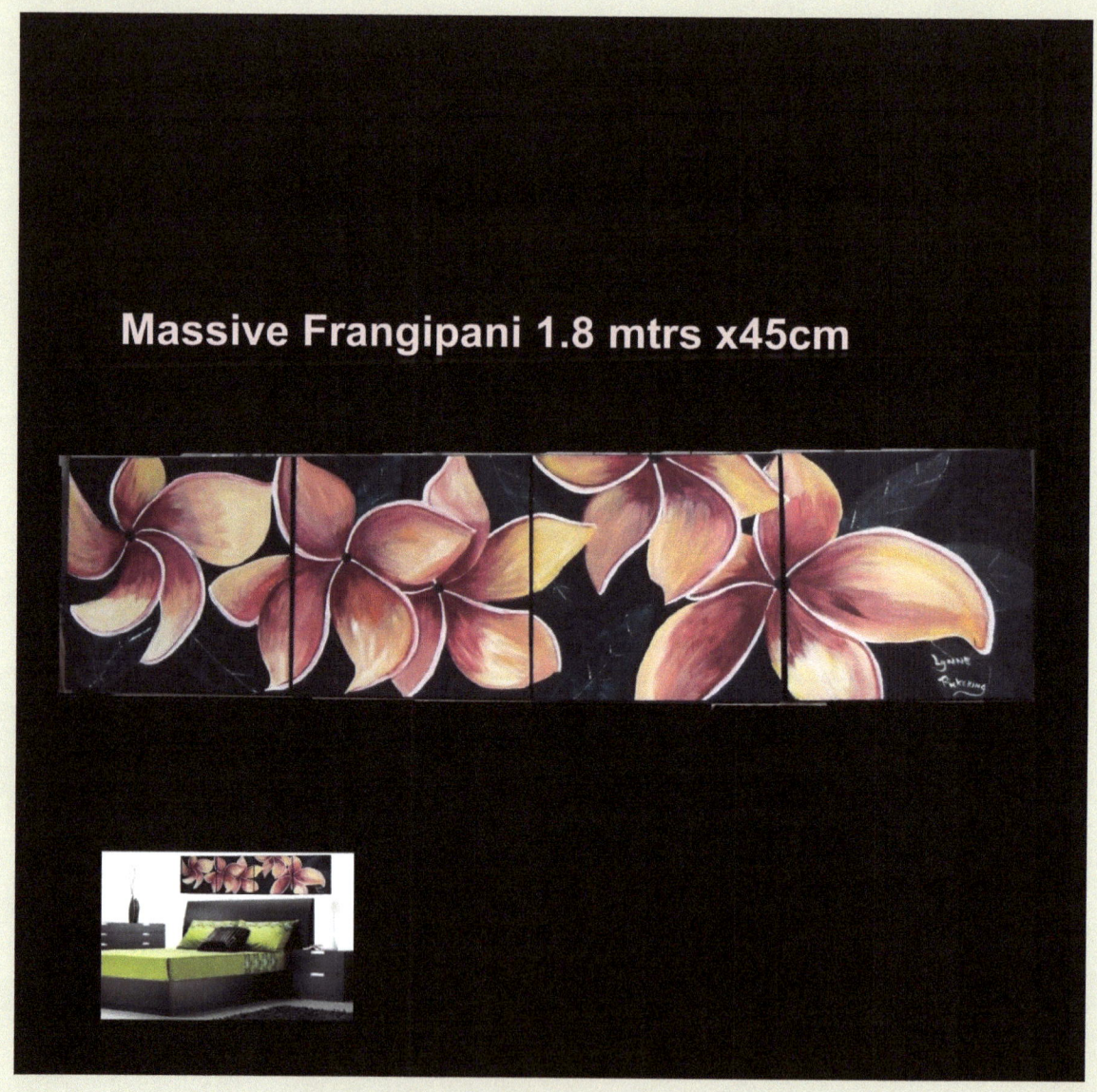

Floral art   red triptych 36 "x36"

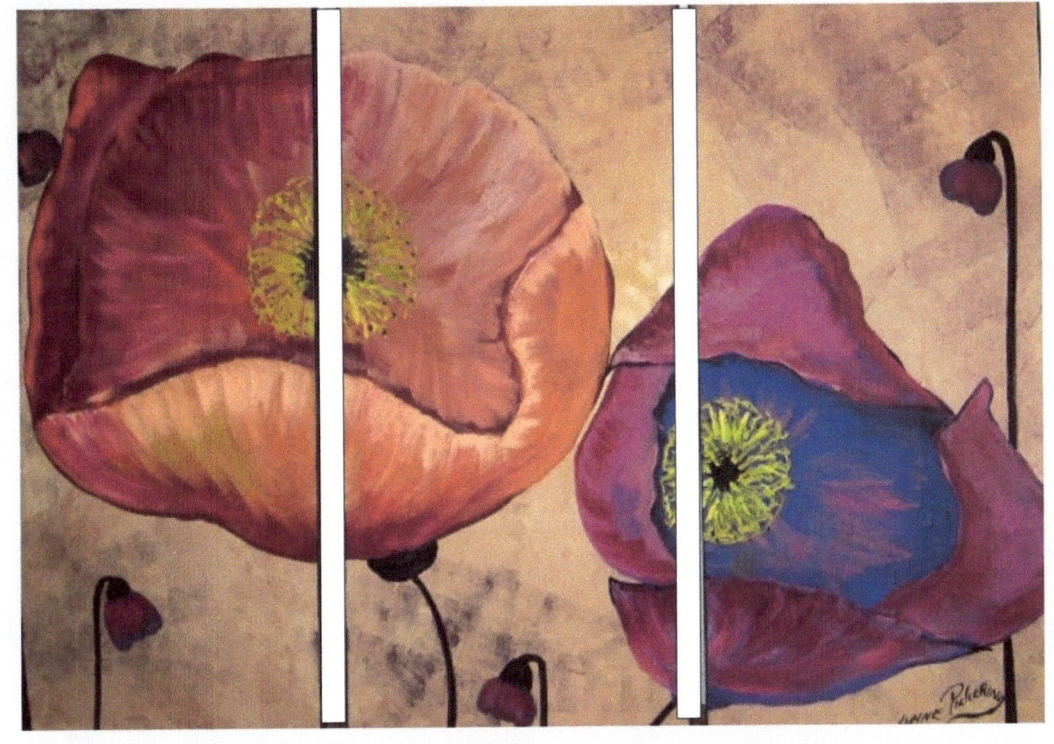

FLORAL THEMES 48"X48" acrylic

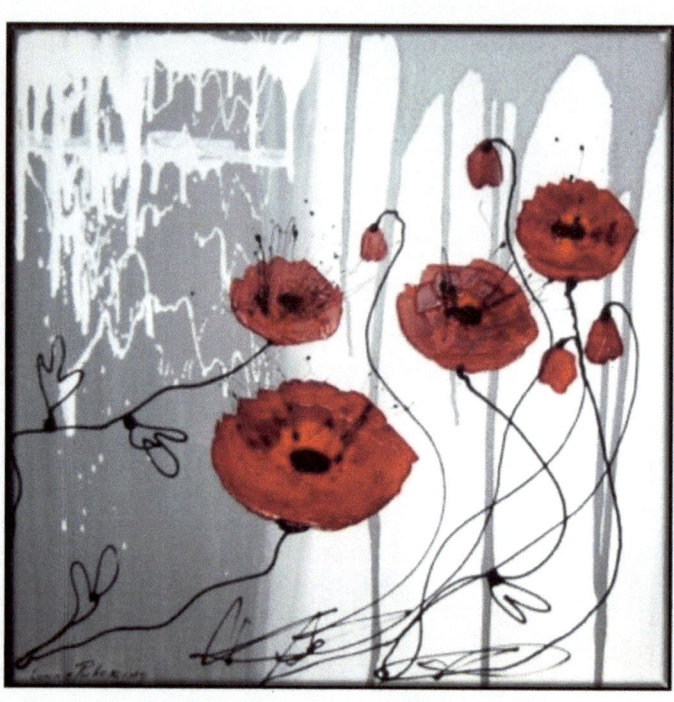

COUNTRY RACES 48"x36" ACRYLIC

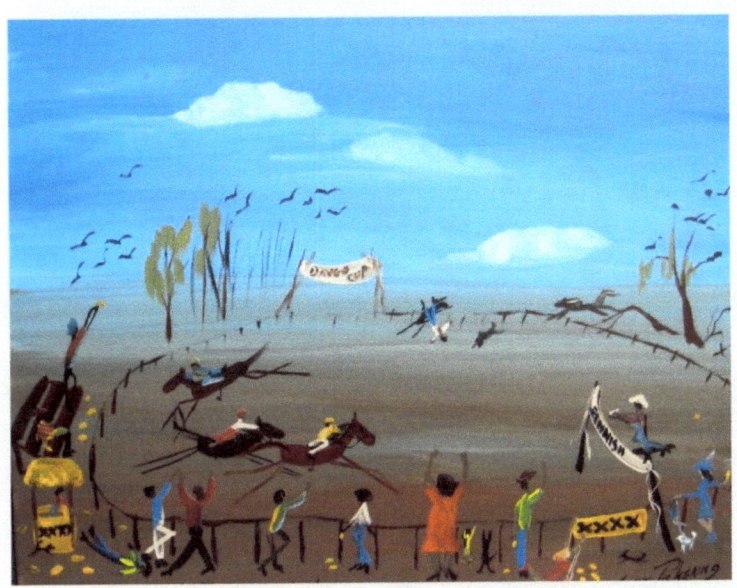

AUSTRALIAN THEME RED PARROTS
48"X36"

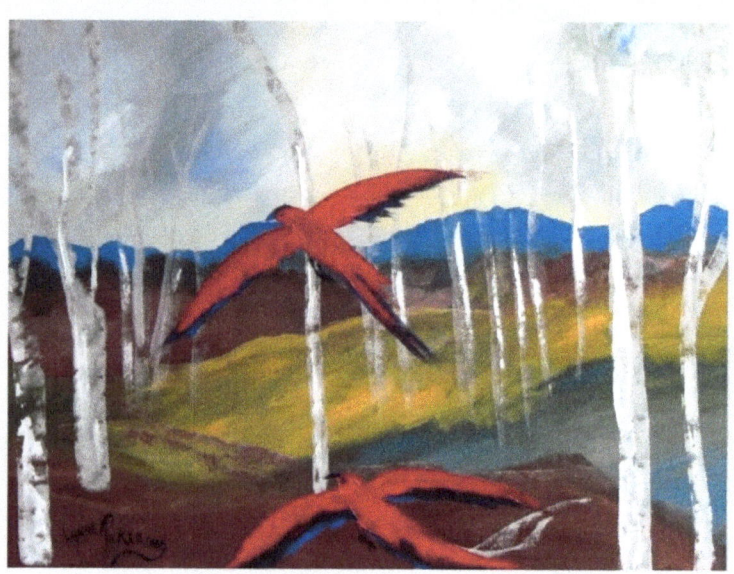

AUSTRALIA OUTBACK THEMES
48"X48" acrylic

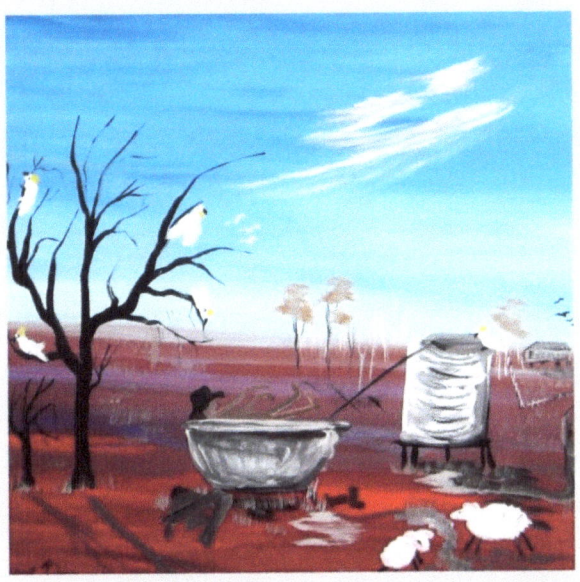

AUSTRALIAN COUNTRY 4FT X3FT acrylic

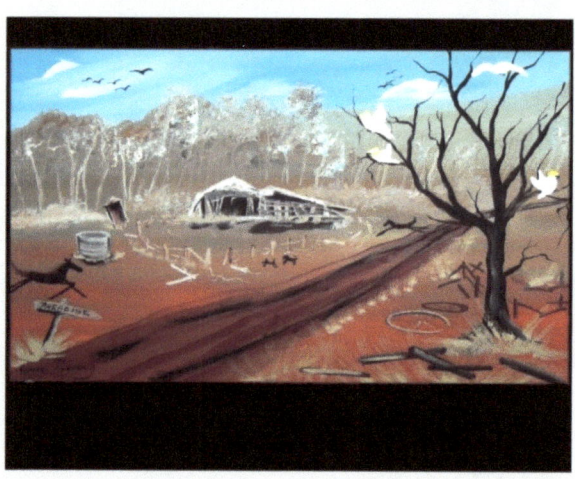

THE FALL 5FTX36" ACRYLIC/MIXED MEDIA OIL

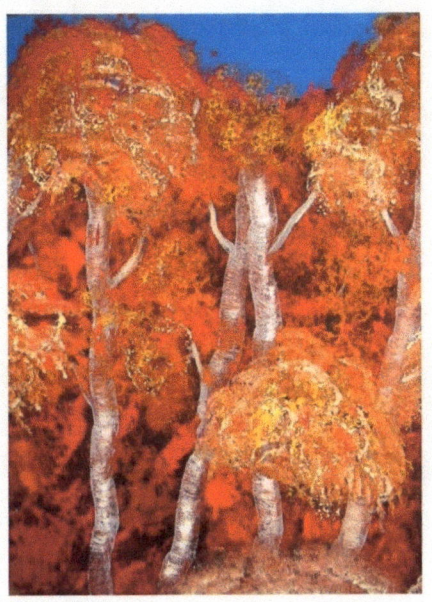

AUSTRALIAN COUNTRY 4FT X3FT acrylic
 MANGROVES

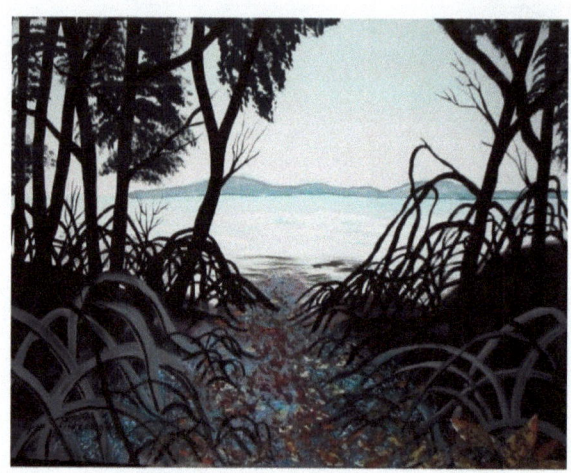

AUSTRALIAN   COBB & COO 36"X36"

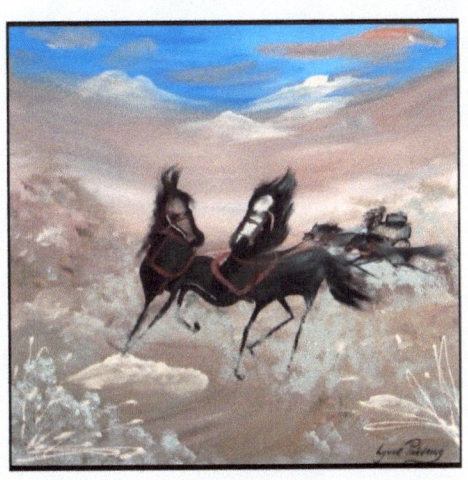

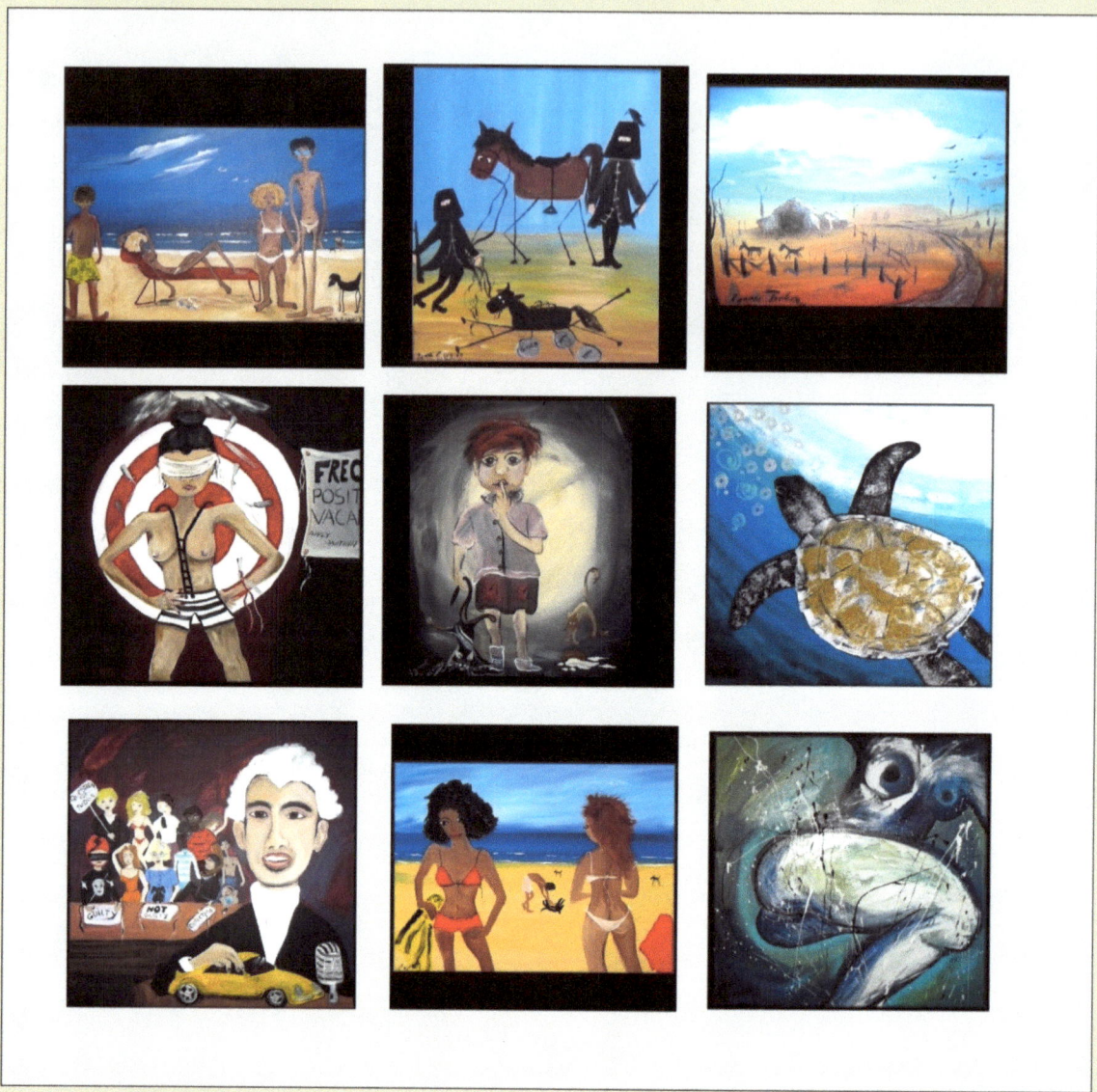

QUIRKY

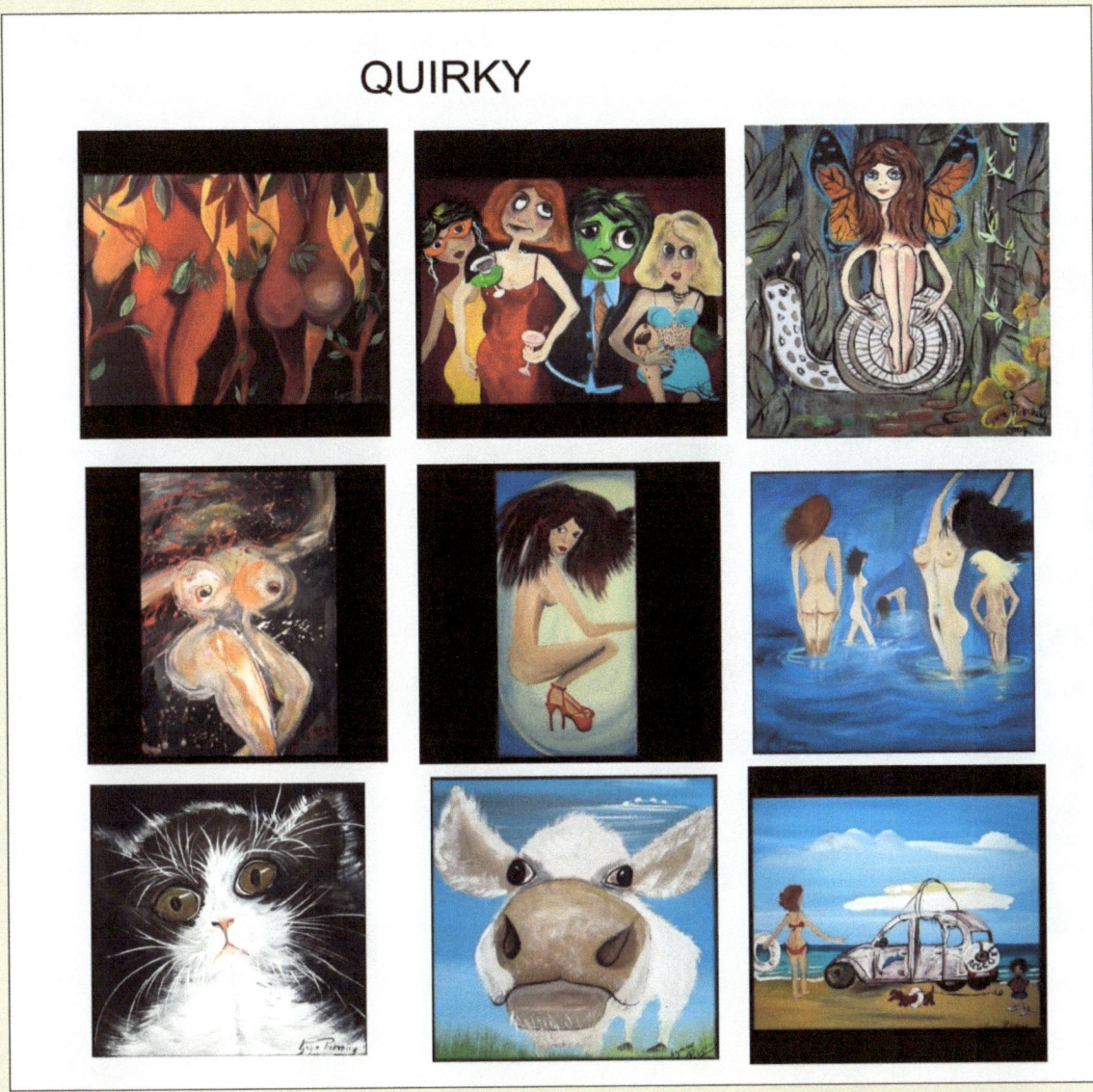

QUIRKY

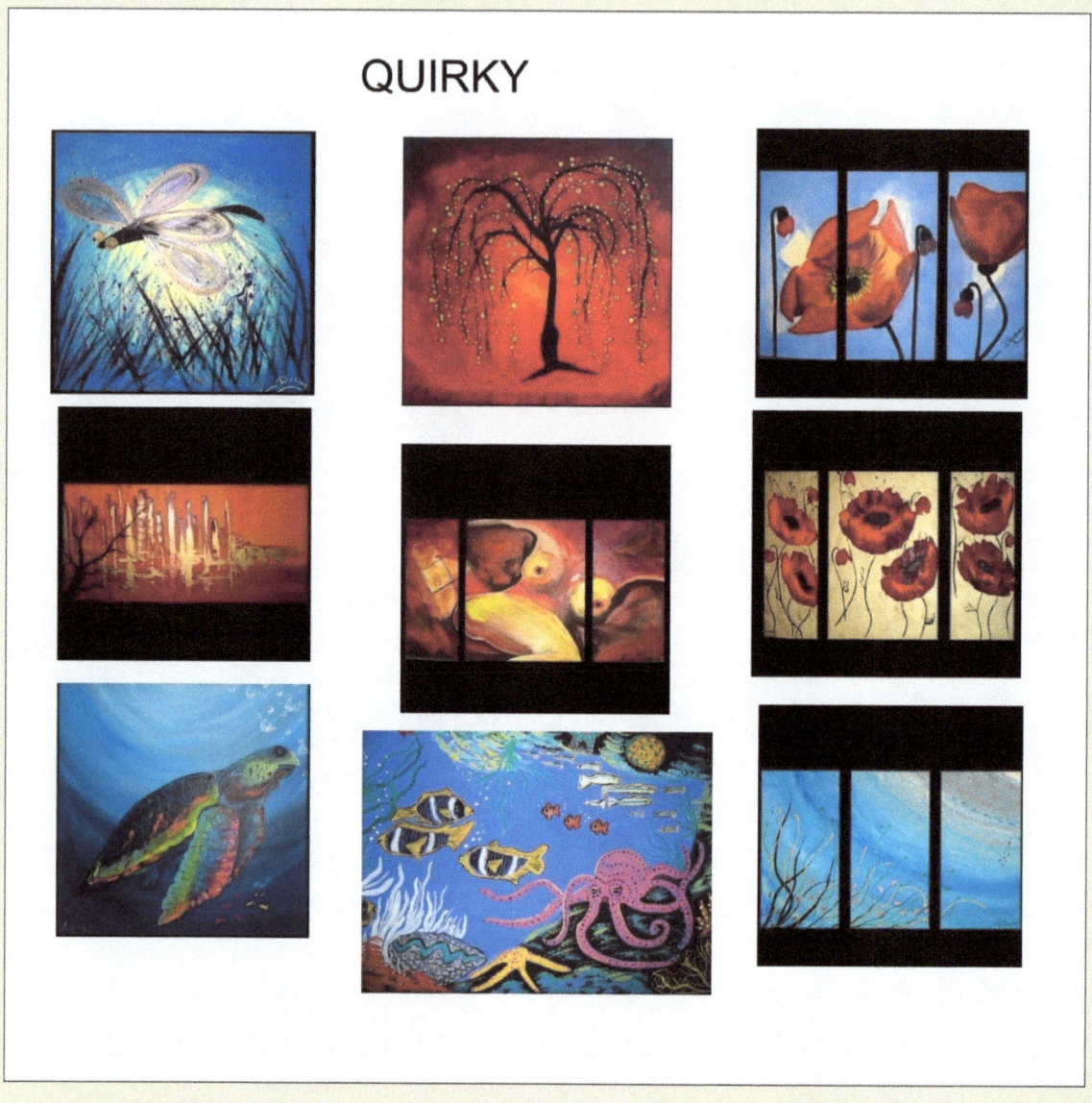

QUIRKY

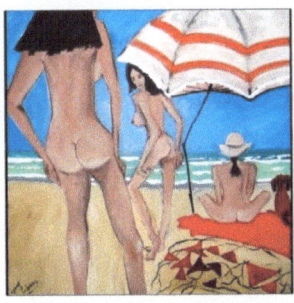 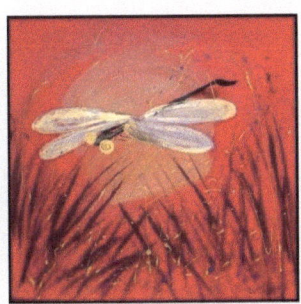 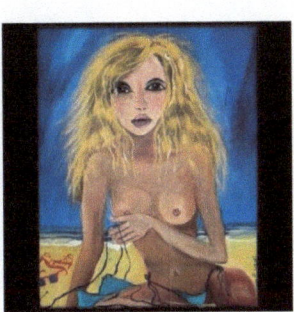

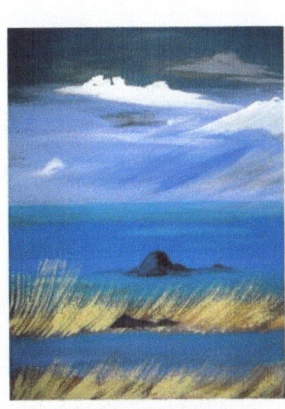 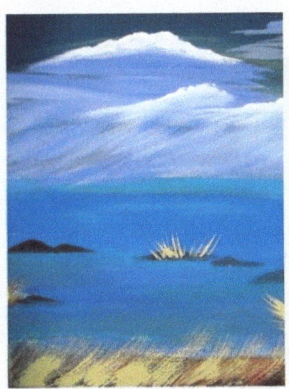 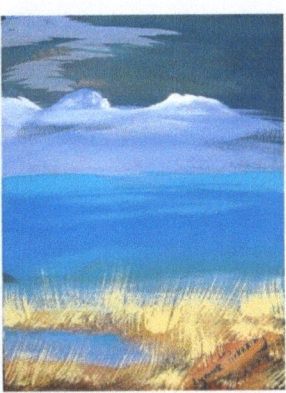

ABSTRACT

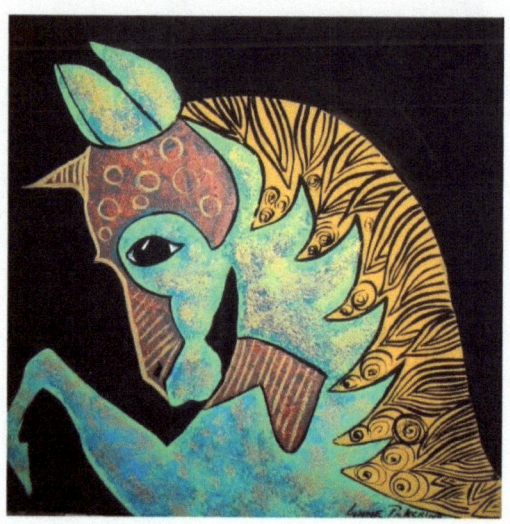

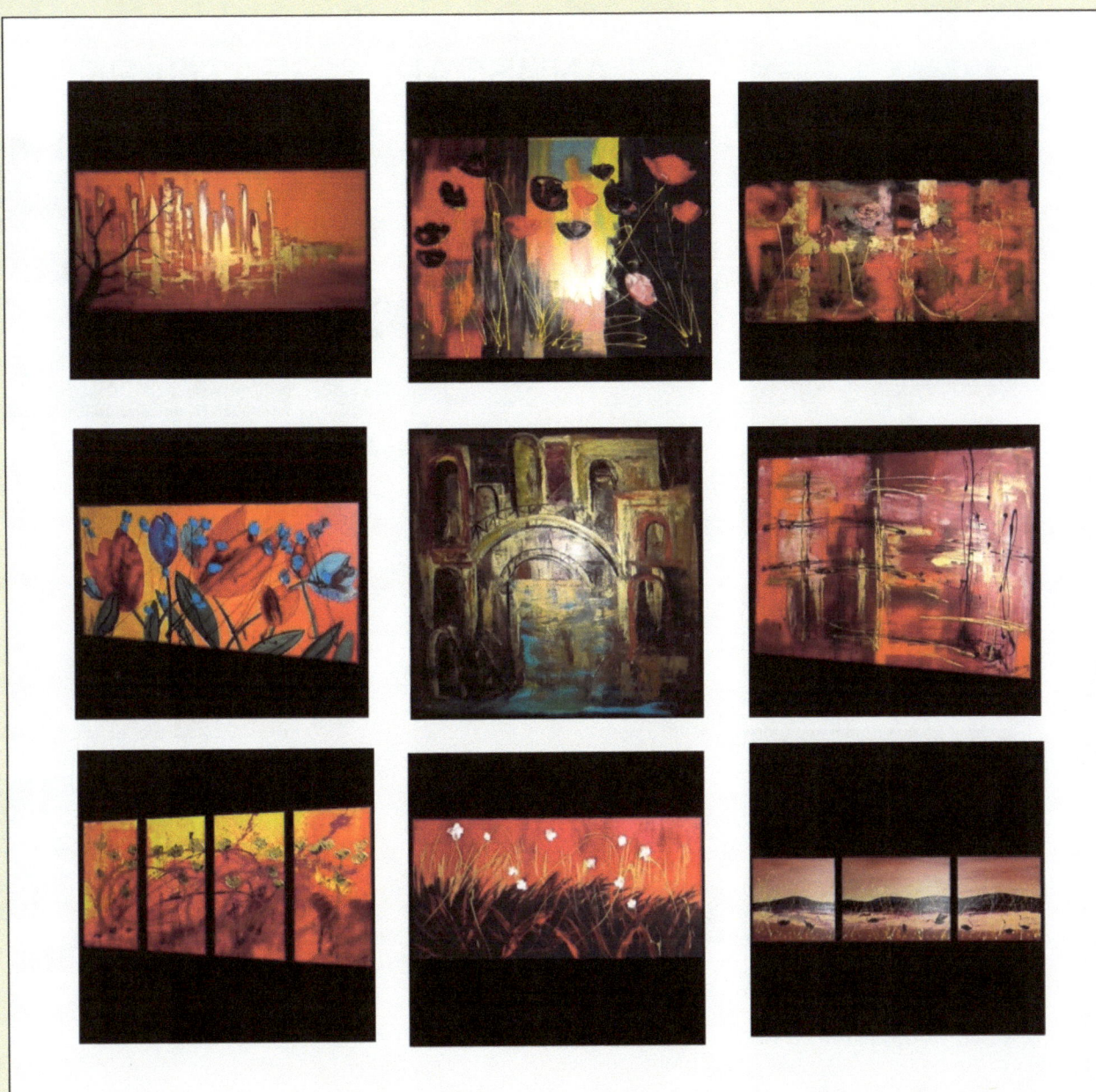

LANDSCAPES SEASCAPES

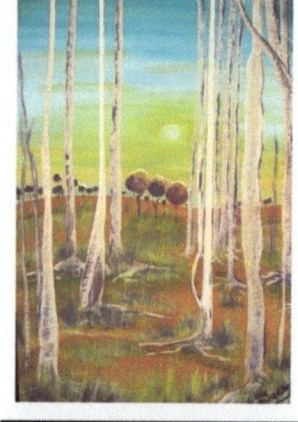
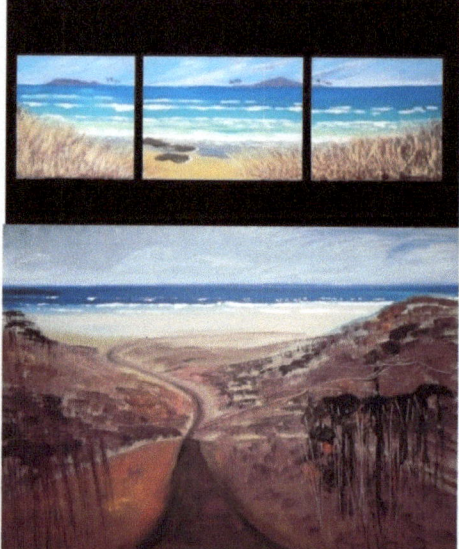
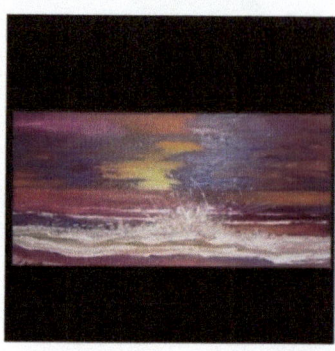
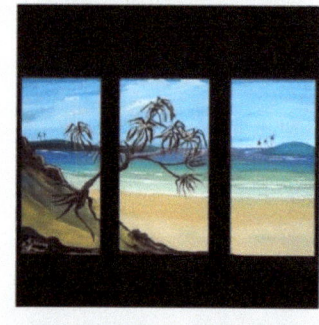
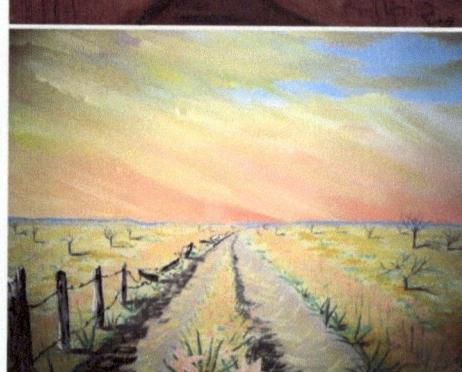
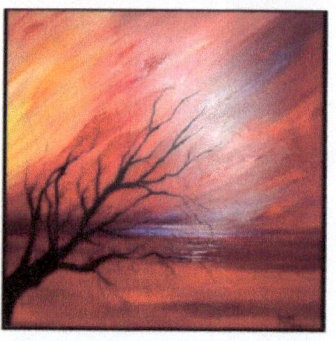
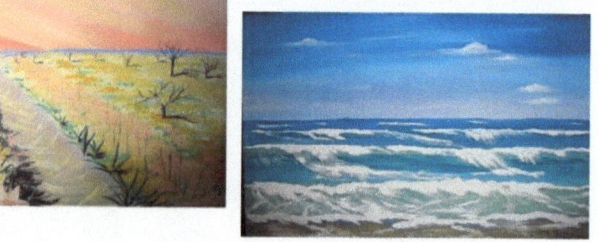

LANDSCAPES

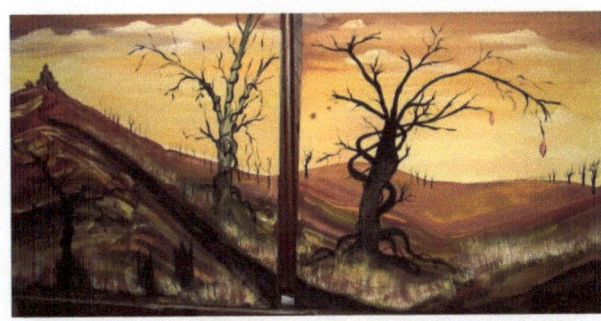

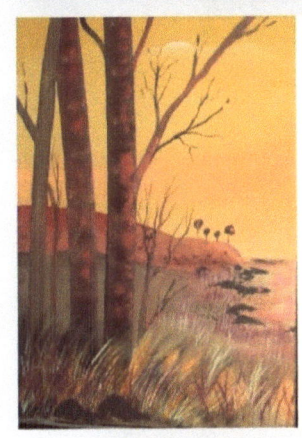
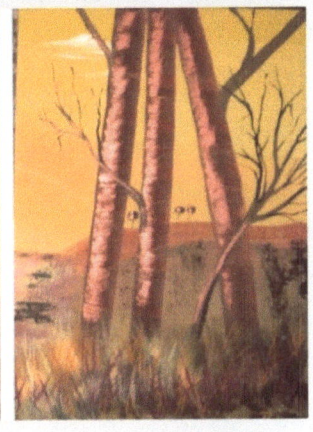

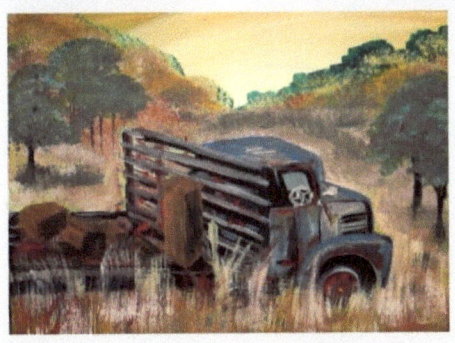

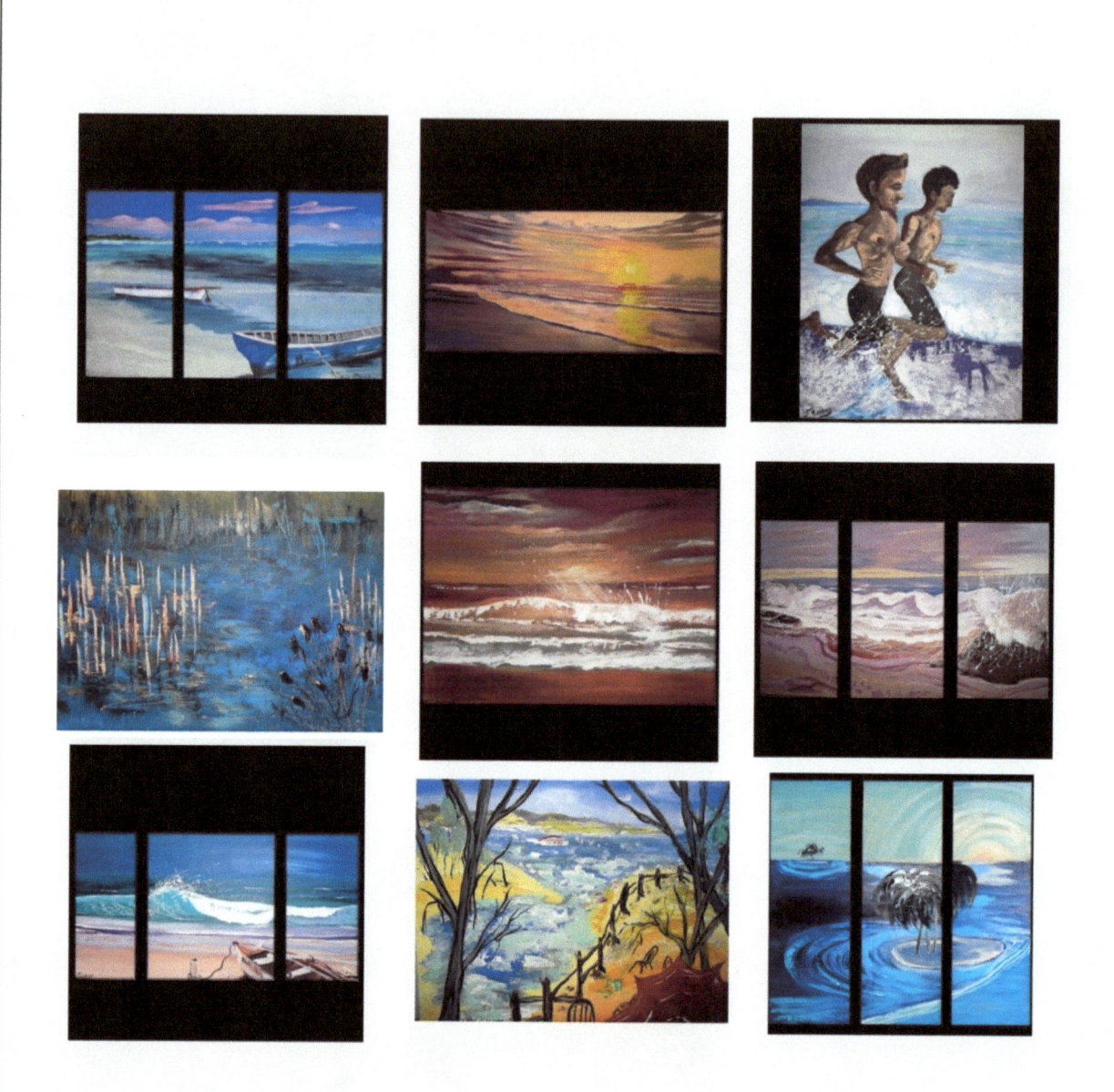